FISHING
AND HOW TO DO IT

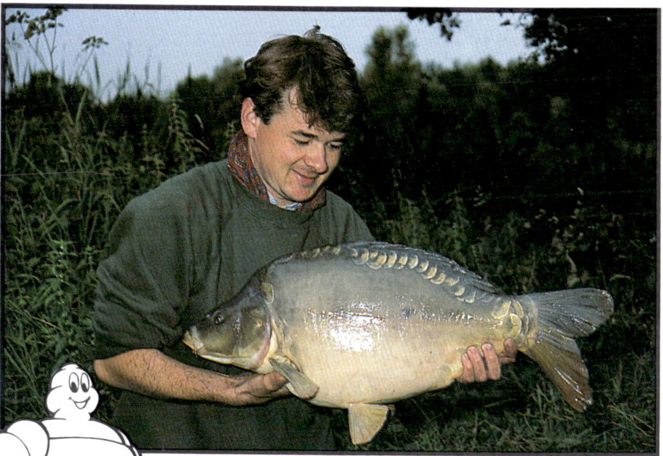

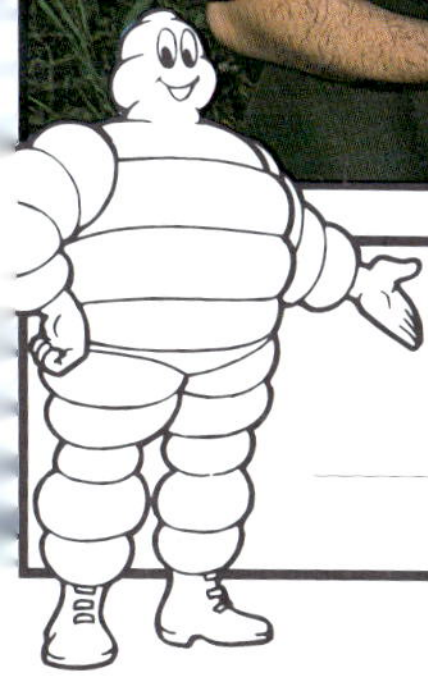

This book belongs to:

TACKLE

Float Rod
A float rod is usually 3-4 metres (10-13 ft) long, built from carbon fibre, with three sections, and it is able to handle lines of 1 kilogram to 2.5 kilograms (2.2 lb-5.3 lb).
I-Spy for **10**

Ledger Rod
When fishing without a float, a ledger rod is used. The best indicators of a bite with this type of rod are a screw-in quiver tip or a swing tip. Which bite indicator is the angler in the photograph using?

I-Spy for **10**
Double with answer

2

TACKLE

Pole Fishing
The tackle used with a pole is very fine and sensitive. The line is fixed directly to the end of the pole, and elastic is used as a shock-absorber.
I-Spy for 15

Spinning Rod
This rod is designed to cast an artificial lure or spinner. Notice the large rings on the rod, and the short handle.
I-Spy for 10

TACKLE

Pike Rod
The pike rod needs to be strong so that it can cast heavy baits such as half a mackerel or a herring. Smaller baits may also be fished — sardines and sprats are popular choices.
I-Spy for 15

Carp Rods
Carp rods are now made from carbon fibre. It is quite common for the carp angler to fish with two rods together. These rods are able to cast bait great distances. What were the first carp rods made from?

I-Spy for 15
Double with answer

TACKLE

Fixed Spool Reel
Great distances can be cast with a fixed spool reel. The line is trapped under the bale arm for winding in, and opened for casting. The spool is interchangeable. True or False?

I-Spy for **5**
Double with answer

Closed Face Reel
The closed face reel has an adjustable clutch or drag, similar to the fixed spool reel, but the line is held under a metal button on this reel instead of by a bale arm. To release the line you touch the reel face.
I-Spy for **10**

Centre Pin Reel
The reel is put to use mainly for 'trotting' a river. The drum of the reel spins freely and so the tackle can be fished with the river's current, and this makes the bait appear to be very natural to the fish.
I-Spy for **15**

5

TACKLE

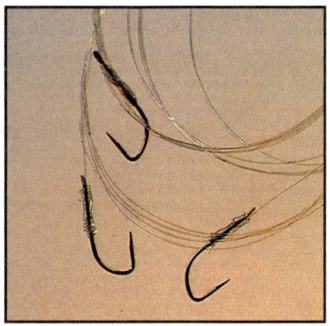

Spade End Hooks to Nylon
These hooks have a flattened end that is whipped to the nylon. You can buy them already tied to nylon or you can do it yourself with the aid of a hook-tying tool. Hooks to nylon are excellent when fishing with maggots or casters.
I-Spy for 5

Barbless Hook
The barbless hook, from size 2 to size 22, can be used for all types of freshwater fishing. The size of a hook is gauged by an even number on a scale of 24 to 2. The higher the number, the smaller the hook. The barbless hook will penetrate better and will do no damage to the fish.
I-Spy for 10

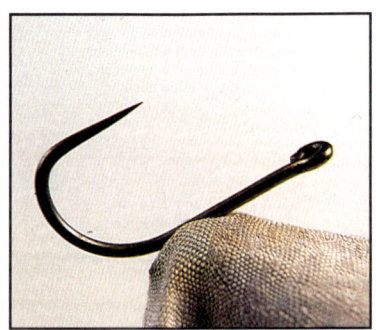

Eyed Hook
A reliable hook is the most important part of the angler's tackle. Eyed hooks rely on a very well-tied knot. A half-blood knot is thought to be one of the best.
I-Spy for 10

TACKLE

Non-toxic Split Shot

These weights are aids to casting and to bait presentation when used beneath a float. Split shot is available in a range of sizes from a tiny No. 12 to a large SSG size. Until quite recently, split shot was made from lead which was toxic. Now, all split shot is a safe, non-toxic material.
I-Spy for 10

Non-toxic Ledger Weights

When ledgering, a choice of weights is available to the angler. They are all designed to aid casting a bait. The most commonly used is the Arlesey Bomb which was invented in the 1950s by Richard Walker, former holder of the caught carp record.
I-Spy for 10

TACKLE

Carp Weights
Carp fishing is often carried out at long range so specialized weights are used. These may have a built-in swivel to prevent the line twisting during long-distance casts. Plastic tubing is also used widely to eliminate tangles.
I-Spy for 15

Olivetti Pole Weights
These were used originally by anglers in continental Europe but they are now commonly available in Britain. Again pole weights are non-toxic. The Olivetti pole weight is shaped like a teardrop and has a hole drilled through it. These leads are fished in conjunction with a pole.

I-Spy for 15

COARSE FISHING FLOATS

The Waggler Float
The waggler float is a useful addition to the tackle box. It is attached to the line by the eye at the base of the float and locked with a split shot. Wagglers are suitable for still water as well as for rivers.
I-Spy for 10

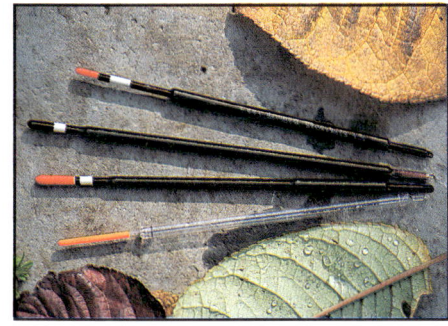

Stick Float
This float is an excellent choice for an angler fishing slow- or medium-flowing water. The classic shotting pattern is to have the largest-size shot nearest the float and gradually reduce the size of the shot towards the hook so that the smallest is nearest the hook.
I-Spy for 10

COARSE FISHING FLOATS

Balsa and Avon Floats
The floats are fished in medium- or fast-flowing water. They are attached to the line using two small collars of silicone rubber that enable the depth at which the float is fished to be changed easily. Avon floats are named after a river. True or False?

*I-Spy for **10**
Double with answer*

The Antenna Float
This float is used for fishing in still or very slow rivers or canals. It is attached to the line by an eyed ring. Antenna floats have their bulk at the bottom whereas river floats are either tapered from the top down or they are straight.
*I-Spy for **5***

The Pole Float
This delicate type of float is used for fishing with a pole. A pole float is often made with a wire stem and it has a fine bristle tip that will indicate the slightest bite.
*I-Spy for **15***

COARSE FISHING FLOATS

Pike Floats
To see a pike float go under is always a thrill. It is important to strike as soon as possible to avoid deep hooking the pike. The float is made from balsa, plastic, or polystyrene. A sunken paternoster is a method of piking using a sunken float.
I-Spy for **10**

Vaned Pike Floats
These are great fun to fish with. As the float can drift the bait aided by the wind across the water, it is necessary to coat your line with a buoyant grease so that it will float too.
I-Spy for **15**

Carp Controller Float
Use one of these floats if you are fishing for carp with a bait floating on the surface. The controller has an eye at the top and its own built-in weight. Try using floating crusts, dog mixer food, or floating boilies for bait.
I-Spy for **10**

11

COARSE FISHING MISCELLANEOUS

Fishing Umbrella
Staying dry can make a fishing trip much more pleasant. The large green fishing umbrella will keep you dry as well as sheltering you from the wind. It is a good idea to tie your umbrella down with guy ropes if it is windy.
I-Spy for 10

The Rod Holdall
Fishing rods can be expensive so it is wise to protect them. Rather than carrying them loose, it is better to use a rod holdall which is carried over the shoulder.
I-Spy for 5

The Bivvy
The bivvy is used when fishing for long periods. It gives excellent protection from the elements. Made of nylon or canvas, it is draped over the fishing umbrella.
I-Spy for 15

COARSE FISHING MISCELLANEOUS

Keep Net
Keep nets are used only by match anglers to retain their catch for recording. Keep nets should be at least 3 metres (10 ft) long. If the net is used in shallow water, a bank stick at the end will keep it spaced out. Never hold fish in a keep net for long periods or they might be damaged.
I-Spy for 5

Landing Net
When a fish is played out, it is time to net it. A landing net is used to lift the fish gently out of the water. Always sink the net below the surface and draw the fish over the net. Do not scoop at the fish. It is better to have a net that is too large than one that is not big enough.
I-Spy for 10

Weighing Scales
It is always exciting to catch a big fish. The exact weight is calculated using a set of scales. Keep a record of your personal best fish for each species.
I-Spy for 10

COARSE FISHING MISCELLANEOUS

Soft Weigh Sling
When you are weighing a specimen fish, you should use a wet soft net weigh sling that is made from a fine, soft mesh. This will protect the fish. Remember to deduct the weight of the sling from the amount shown on the scales.
I-Spy for 10

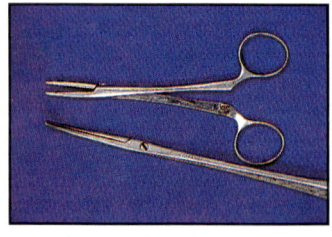

↑ Forceps
Forceps are used for unhooking a fish, such as a pike, that has a bony mouth, or a carp that has leathery lips. Forceps are made from stainless steel that will not rust.
I-Spy for 5

Unhooking Mat
This is a foam mat that will prevent the fish from being damaged if it should flap on the bank. If you are photographing a specimen capture, it is always best to kneel down and have the mat under the fish. Never stand up with a specimen fish in case you drop it.
I-Spy for 10

COARSE FISHING MISCELLANEOUS

Disgorger
The disgorger is used for unhooking a deeply hooked fish. To use it, hold the fish carefully but firmly behind the gills. Hold the line tightly and slide the disgorger down it. Release the hook gently and remove it with the disgorger.
I-Spy for 5

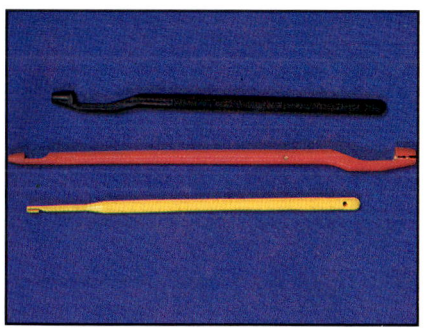

Catapult
The catapult is used to put loose feed into a baited area. Maggots, casters, groundbait, or boilies are some of the baits that can be fired with a catapult.
I-Spy for 10

Rod Rest
The rod rest is screwed into a bank stick that is pushed firmly into the ground. After casting, the rod is placed on the rod rest. It is a good idea to have a front rod rest with a 'V' or a groove cut so that the line is not trapped.
I-Spy for 5

COARSE FISHING MISCELLANEOUS

Bite Alarm
The bite alarm or 'buzzer' is popular with carp anglers. When a fish moves the line, the alarm will bleep alerting the angler to the bite.
I-Spy for 15

↓ Drop Back Indicator
This type of bite indicator is designed for the pike angler. The line is held under tension in a clip. When the pike picks up the bait, the orange ball will drop back to signal the bite. Always strike as soon as possible.
I-Spy for 15

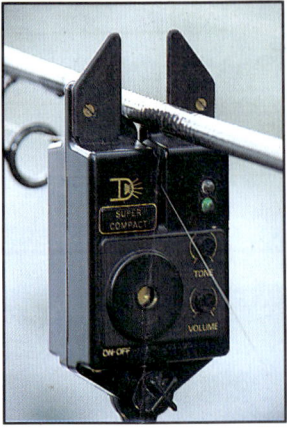

↓ Quiver Tip
If the angler screws a quiver tip into the end of the rod, it provides a very sensitive method of bite indication. It is ideally suited to river fishing. The line is pulled tight to the tip so that any movement is shown.
I-Spy for 5

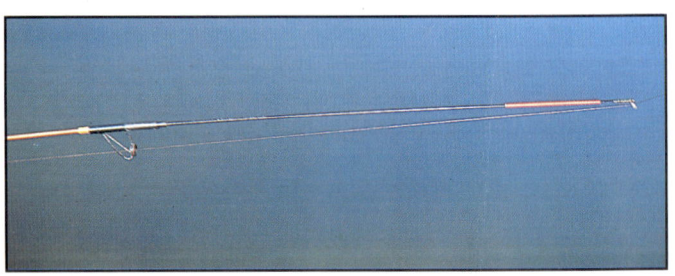

COARSE FISHING MISCELLANEOUS

Swing Tip
The swing tip is a reliable way of detecting a bite. It is screwed on to the tip ring and, after casting out, it is allowed to hang down. The tip will swing up when a fish bites. A swing tip is used when float fishing.
True or False?
I-Spy for 5
Double with answer

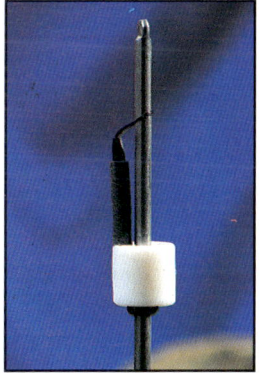

↑ Monkey Climber
The monkey climber is often used in conjunction with an electronic bite alarm. It consists of a metal needle and a plastic body or 'monkey'. The monkey slides up the needle when a fish bites.
I-Spy for 10

← Bait Dropper
On a fast-flowing, or deep, river, a bait dropper is used to put loose bait on the river bed. The dropper is loaded with your chosen bait, cast out, and lowered to the bottom of the river. As it drops, it releases its contents.
I-Spy for 10

17

COARSE FISHING MISCELLANEOUS

Swimfeeder
The swimfeeder is an ideal means to attract fish to your bait. It is a small plastic container with holes in it. It is loaded with maggots which escape through the holes close to the hook bait. Can a swimfeeder be used in a lake as well as in a river?

*I-Spy for **10***
Double with answer

Plummet
You can use a plummet to find out the exact depth of the water where you are planning to fish. In this way, you can set your float at the right depth. The hook is passed through the ring and pushed into the cork. Carefully plummet the depth before you start fishing.
I-Spy for 5

Beads
Beads prevent tangles and protect knots from damage. A bead is threaded on to the line between a weight and a swivel.
I-Spy for 5

COARSE FISHING MISCELLANEOUS

Swivel
To prevent your line becoming twisted, you should use a swivel. The three main types of swivel are: the snap link; the barrel; and the three-way. It is essential to use a swivel when using a spinner.
I-Spy for **10**

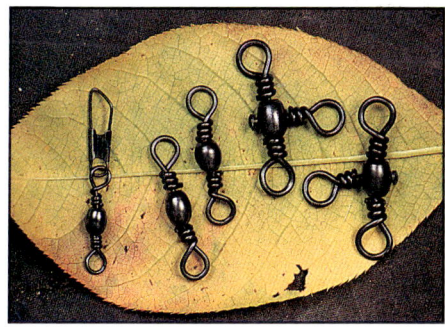

Hair Rig
The hair rig is a recent innovation. It consists of a short length of nylon dacron with the hook at one end. A small loop or 'hair' is tied to the eye or shank of the hook. The bait is then passed on to the hair with a needle. This is a good rig for carp fishing.
I-Spy for **15**

Wire Trace
When fishing for pike a wire trace is used to prevent the fish using its sharp teeth to bite through the line. Treble hooks are attached close together, and a swivel is fixed to the other end of the trace. Always strike early with this set-up.
I-Spy for **15**

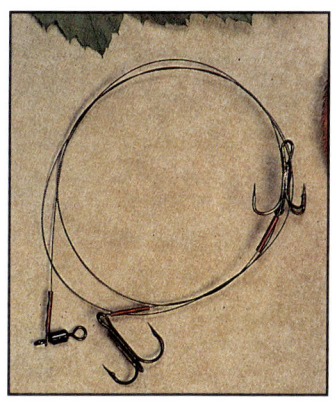

COARSE FISHING MISCELLANEOUS

Braided Hooklinks
Another type of line is dacron which is braided and extremely supple, so that it is difficult for the fish to detect it. Wary fish, such as carp, may often be caught with a soft hooklink.
*I-Spy for **10***

Nylon Monofilament Line
Nylon line is supplied in a range of strengths or breaking strains. Although it looks very fine, it is extremely strong. Never leave any unwanted nylon line on the bankside because it could be a danger to wildlife.
*I-Spy for **5***

Waders
In shallow water, it can be an advantage to wade out to reach the fish. There are two types of waders — thigh waders and chest waders. Chest waders are usually worn by the salmon angler who stands in midstream.
*I-Spy **10** for each type of wader*

COARSE FISHING BAITS

Maggots
Maggots are the most popular of all coarse fishing baits. A wide variety of fish can be caught using maggots. They are available in many different colours and are best used by hooking the blunt end on to the hook.
I-Spy for **5**

Casters
The grub or maggot of a fly develops into a chrysalis or caster. Fresh casters are a good bait for roach as well as for bream, chub, and dace. A proven method is to conceal a size 16 or 18 hook in a single caster.
I-Spy for **10**

COARSE FISHING BAITS

Groundbait
When mixed with water and fed in small balls, a groundbait will often draw fish into an area. Try adding casters or maggots to the groundbait. Bream and tench will respond well to groundbaiting.
I-Spy for 10

Worms
Worms are a cheap and easy-to-use bait which will catch all species of freshwater fishes. The three types of worms used for fishing are: lobworms; brandlings; and redworms. A good bait for bream is a small redworm tipped with a caster.
I-Spy for 5

Sweetcorn
Its bright colour and sweet juice make sweetcorn a very convenient bait. It will catch carp, tench, bream, and chub. A single grain can be fished on a size 14 hook, or you could try three grains on a size 10.
I-Spy for 10

COARSE FISHING BAITS

Cheese
Another bait to be found in the supermarket is cheese. This can be fished in a small cube or as a paste. Leave the hookpoint exposed because cheese hardens in water. Cheese is a good river bait for chub and roach.
I-Spy for **10**

Bread
If you use floating bread crust to fish for carp near lily pads, it is exciting to see the fish rise and take the bait. Bread flake or paste on a size 12 hook is an excellent bait for chub or roach. The flake should be just lightly pinched on to the hook so that it stays fluffy.
I-Spy for **10**

23

COARSE FISHING BAITS

Luncheon Meat
Luncheon meat, cut into cubes, is a successful bait, particularly if you are trying to catch barbel and chub. Try fishing luncheon meat with a ledger in a weir pool. Watch out for the bite because it will often be a sudden strong pull on the rod tip.
I-Spy for 10

Boilies
Boilies are small balls of bait which are flavoured, coloured, and boiled. Boiling the bait gives it a tough skin, preventing small fishes from eating it. More big carp are caught on boilies and hair rigs than any other bait.
I-Spy for 10

COARSE FISHING BAITS

Chick Peas
Chick peas make a cheap particle bait. They are best bought dry and then soaked in water until they are soft. They can be flavoured and coloured easily or fished just as they are.
I-Spy for 10

Hemp
Hemp is a fine seed bait that can be used as a hookbait for roach or fed into a swim as groundbait. Try putting a bed of hemp into the swim and fishing a larger bait, such as luncheon meat, on top of it.
I-Spy for 10

COARSE FISHING BAITS

Sardine
The bright-silver sea fish, the sardine, is a perfect-sized bait, used whole, for pike fishing. It should be fished either under a pike float or freelined on the bottom. Fish for pike with a wire trace.
I-Spy for 5

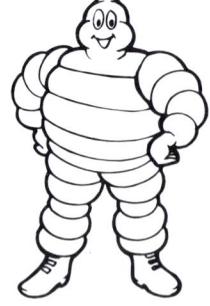

Mackerel
Freelined on a wire trace, an oily mackerel cut in half will catch pike. A half herring can also be fished using this method. A strong pike rod is needed to cast these baits.
I-Spy for 10

COARSE FISHING BAITS

Plugs

A plug is an artificial lure that is cast out and retrieved. Most have a vane at the head that will make the plug dive. Plugs have an irresistible wobble that urges the predatory fish to attack. Pike, perch, and chub can be caught on plugs. Would you use a spinning rod to cast a plug?
I-Spy for **10** — double with answer

Spinners and Spoons

Designed to imitate small fishes, these metal lures have treble hooks and swivels attached to them. Cast out a spoon and wind it back with a sink-and-draw action using a light spinning rod for good sport.
I-Spy for **10**

COARSE FISHES

Pike

The pike is the largest predatory coarse fish. It has a lean, powerful body, bony head, and sharp, slanting teeth. It can reach the awesome weight of 18 kilograms (40 lb) if there are vast shoals of fodder fish available in the water.

Small pike are known as jacks. True or False?
I-Spy for 10 — double with answer _____

Mirror Carp

Carp are cunning and strong — always a prized catch. The scattered scaling on the mirror carp is very distinctive. Britain's biggest rod-caught fish is a mirror carp of 23.4 kilograms (51½ lb), caught by Christopher Yates in 1980.
I-Spy for 20

COARSE FISHES

Common Carp
The fully scaled carp can grow to the same enormous size as the mirror carp. Indeed, the carp record of 20 kilograms (44 lb) was held for many years by a famous common carp, caught and named Clarissa, by the legendary angler, Richard Walker. From where was Walker's record carp caught?
*I-Spy for **15** — double with answer* _____

Crucian Carp
The Crucian carp does not grow as large as the common or the mirror carp. Unlike the common carp, the Crucian carp has no barbels on its mouth. It is the same golden colour, though, and it is fully scaled. This fish is a determined fighter and found in still waters.
*I-Spy for **15***

29

COARSE FISHES

↑ Rudd
The rudd is a beautiful golden fish with deep-red fins. It is a surface feeder. Look closely at the lower lip — it protrudes beyond the upper lip. A rudd of over 1 kilogram (2¼ lb) is a very special specimen. The rudd's habitat is the still waters of lakes and ponds.
I-Spy for **20**

↓ Roach
Small roach and rudd can be confused with each other. The roach is silver in colour, and its mouth is in a central position unlike the upturned mouth of the rudd. Roach are more widespread and are found in all kinds of rivers as well as still waters.
I-Spy for **10**

COARSE FISHES

Dace
The dace is one of the smaller fishes that inhabit British waters. Small dace and chub are similar in appearance but the dace has concave dorsal and oral fins whereas those of the chub are convex.
I-Spy for **10**

Chub
Although the chub is known mainly as a river fish, it will also thrive in still water. Easy to I-Spy, with its large mouth and thick lips, the scales are large and edged with black. Chub can be tempted with many different baits: try cheese, maggots, or a freelined slug.
I-Spy for **10**

COARSE FISHES

↑ Barbel
With the four barbels on its upper lip, the barbel is easily identified. As it hovers over the river bed, the fish uses its barbels to locate its food among the stones and gravel. It is a strong fighting fish and it is often tempted with a cube of luncheon meat.
I-Spy for **20**

↓ Perch
The beautiful, stripy backed perch inhabits rivers as well as still water. It can be caught using a variety of methods from a small spinn to a bunch of worms. Try fishing deeper holes or slacks in the river to locate the perch.
I-Spy for **10**

COARSE FISHES

Bream
The deep-bodied bream is a bottom-feeding fish. This shoal fish frequents still water or slower rivers. Groundbait is often used to keep bream in a swim.
I-Spy for **10**

Tench
The olive-green tench is often found in still water. When the British coarse fishing season opens on 16 June each year, the tench is the popular quarry. Favourite baits for this fish are sweetcorn, boilies, and bread.
I-Spy for **15**

33

TYPES OF WATER

Small River
Rivers change in size as they flow from their source to the sea. The flow will be faster in a shallow river, and the fishes will include chub, dace, roach, and barbel.
I-Spy for **10**

Wide, Slow River
As the river flows to its lower reaches, it will widen and deepen. Here you are more likely to find bream, perch, and roach. A swimfeeder is a good method on this type of water.
I-Spy for **10**

Small Stillwater
Cast a bait near to weeds or lily pads where there is natural cover and food for the fishes. Carp and tench will not be far away. Early morning is often a good fishing time.
I-Spy for **10**

TYPES OF WATER

Large Lake
Finding the fish can be a problem in a large lake. Clouds of silt or patches of bubbles are signs of feeding fishes. Visit your local lake at dawn to I-Spy them. A good pair of binoculars and dark sunglasses will help you to locate them.
I-Spy for **15**

Gravel Pit
Gravel pits offer good fishing opportunities although they can be a daunting prospect because of their size and variations in depth. Most species of coarse fishes will inhabit the gravel pit. Try for carp, tench, and bream in the summer, and pike in the winter months.
I-Spy for **10**

Weir Pool
The river is well oxygenated by the strong flow of water below the weir. Fishes are attracted to this. The main species in weir pools are barbel and chub although it is always worth a cast with a spinner or a plug for pike or perch.
I-Spy for **15**

35

TYPES OF WATER

Reservoir
Reservoirs supply our homes with water. Many are created by building a dam across a valley and flooding it. The newly formed lake may be stocked with trout so that it is a popular fishery.
I-Spy for **15**

Swans
Swans live on and near the water, and they are found on many lakes and rivers. Never leave any discarded line, hooks, or weights on the ground because these could all seriously harm these beautiful birds.
I-Spy for **10**

GAME FISHING

Small Trout Fishery
Stocked with rainbow and brown trout, these artificial lakes are often gravel pits and offer good fly fishing for trout. Sometimes, very large trout are stocked, so that the sport is exciting. This type of water has produced the record rainbow trout. True or False?

I-Spy for 15
Double with answer

Fly Fishing
An artificial fly is used to catch salmon and trout. The fly is cast with a fly line that is balanced exactly to the rod. The fly is cast out and then pulled or twitched back to entice the fish to take it.
I-Spy for 15

GAME FISHING

Boat Fishing
Trout will often rise to the surface to feed; drifting from a boat will put the angler among the fishes. When fishing from a boat, long-distance casts are not so vital to find the fish.
I-Spy for 15

Fly Lines
There are two basic types of fly line: one which floats and one which sinks. The floating fly line is used to present a dry fly on the surface. The wet fly line is sinking and is fished with a nymph lure or a wet fly.
I-Spy 10 for each

Fly Reel
The fly reel is attached to the fly rod at the very end of the handle. The line is pulled off the reel before the cast, and it is the forward and backward motion of the rod and line that casts the fly.
I-Spy for 10

GAME FISHING

Trout Flies
The fly is made from fur and feather whipped on to a hook. Some, such as the dry fly or nymph, actually resemble living insects. Most other wet flies or lures are made to imitate nothing at all but are irresistible to the trout. There is a fly tied to imitate the daddy long legs. True or False?
I-Spy for 15 — double with answer _____

Salmon Flies
Salmon flies are tied on to larger hooks than trout flies are. Many successful salmon flies have bright blues, oranges, and yellows in them. A popular early season lure is the prawn imitation.
I-Spy for 15

39

GAME FISHING

Fly Tying
A fly-tying vice is used to hold the hook in place, and the fly, lure, or nymph is then built up out of fur, feather, wool, and tinsel tied in with silk. An easy fly to start with is the black and peacock spider.
I-Spy for **10**

Brown Trout
This fish naturally inhabits fast-flowing streams and rivers, but it is also bred and stocked into trout fisheries. Fishing with an artificial fly is an enjoyable way to catch the brown trout.
I-Spy for **15**

GAME FISHING

Rainbow Trout
Most artificial trout fisheries contain the rainbow trout. These fishes are reared in cages and pens and stocked into the lake for fly anglers to catch. The rainbow trout has a silvery body with a pinkish sheen. This fish is a member of the salmon family.
I-Spy for 15

Salmon
Salmon migrate from the sea into the cleanest of our rivers to spawn. Salmon fishing is an expensive sport. The fish can be caught on large artificial flies, shrimps, or lures.
I-Spy for 25

SEA ANGLING

Shore Fishing
Sea fishing from the shore is best at high tide or on the rising tide. In the course of each twenty-four hour period, there are two high tides and two low tides. Piers and harbour walls are fruitful fishing places.
I-Spy for 10

Boat Fishing
When fishing from a boat, a short, strong rod made from fibre glass or carbon fibre is best. The tackle is lowered straight down from the boat around a wreck, for example. Wrecks of sunken ships often make very good fishing areas because they attract large numbers of fish.
I-Spy for 10

SEA ANGLING

Multiplier Reel
The multiplier reel is designed to retrieve line rapidly. It is fished on top of the rod. It can be used for distance casting from the shore or in conjunction with a boat rod and nylon monofilament line.
I-Spy for **15**

Beach-casting Rod
This rod is designed to hurl the baited hook and lead more than 150 metres (500 ft). This powerfully built rod has a long handle and large rings. Bite detection is by watching the rod tip for knocks.
I-Spy for **15**

43

SEA ANGLING

Sea Floats
Float fishing from a harbour wall, using simple float tackle, will tempt mackerel, wrasse, flatfish, and mullet. A variety of baits will give results; try mackerel strips, rag worm, or lug worm.
I-Spy for 10

Lug Worm
The lug worm is eaten by most of our sea fishes. Lug worm can easily be dug from the beach at low tide. I-Spy the worm casts in the sand and then dig around them with a fork.
I-Spy for 15

Sandeel
Bass and pollock are both taken on this bait. It is possible to buy frozen sandeels, or to collect your own live sandeels from the shallow water of sandy estuaries.
I-Spy for 15

44

SEA ANGLING

Rubber Eel
These elongated rubber lures are excellent for reef or wreck fishing where the target fishes are pollock or coalfish. Red is the most popular colour.
I-Spy for **10**

Feathers
Once a shoal of mackerel has been located, it is quite easy to land several at a time on a string of brightly coloured feathers.
I-Spy for **5**

45

SEA ANGLING

Sea Leads
A variety of leads is available to the sea angler. For beach casting, the torpedo-shaped lead is designed to cast the maximum distance. Always use a good swivel with the lead to prevent the line twisting.
I-Spy for **5**

Mackerel
The mackerel has a vivid blue-and-black mottled back and bright-silver sides. It may be caught from the shore and from boats. It is a hard fighting fish for its size. What is a small mackerel called?

I-Spy for **15**
Double with answer

SEA ANGLING

Mullet
The mullet is caught close to the shore from harbours and from piers. It will also travel up estuaries where a delicate approach with a light float tackle and bread will give good sport.
I-Spy for 20

Wrasse
Wrasse live among the rocks and reefs along our coastline. The largest and most regularly caught type is the ballan wrasse.
I-Spy for 20

INDEX

Bait Dropper 17
Barbel 32
Beads 18
Bite Alarm 16
Bivvy 12
Boat Fishing 38, 42
Boilies 24
Bread 23
Bream 33
Carp, Common 29
Carp, Crucian 29
Carp, Mirror 28
Casters 21
Catapult 15
Cheese 23
Chick Peas 25
Chub 31
Dace 31
Disgorger 15
Drop Back Indicator 16
Eel, Rubber 45
Feathers 45
Fishing Umbrella 12
Flies, Salmon 39
Flies, Trout 39
Float, Antenna 10
Float, Carp Controller 11
Float, Pole 10
Float, Stick 9
Float, Waggler 9
Floats, Balsa and Avon 10
Floats, Pike 11
Floats, Sea 44
Floats, Vaned Pike 11
Fly Fishing 37
Fly Tying 40
Forceps 14
Gravel Pit 35
Groundbait 22
Hair Rig 19
Hemp 25
Hook, Barbless 6
Hook, Eyed 6
Hooklinks, Braided 20
Keep Net 13
Lake, Large 35
Landing Net 13
Leads, Sea 46
Line, Nylon Monofilament 20
Lines, Fly 38
Luncheon Meat 24
Mackerel 26, 46
Maggots 21
Monkey Climber 17
Mullet 47
Perch 32
Pike 28
Plugs 27
Plummet 18
Pole Fishing 3
Quiver Tip 16
Reel, Centre Pin 5
Reel, Closed Face 5
Reel, Fixed Spool 5
Reel, Fly 38
Reel, Multiplier 43
Reservoir 36
River, Small 34
River, Wide Slow 34
Roach 30
Rod Holdall 12
Rod Rest 15
Rod, Beach-casting 43
Rod, Float 2
Rod, Ledger 2
Rod, Pike 4
Rod, Spinning 3
Rods, Carp 4
Rudd 30
Salmon 41
Sandeel 44
Sardine 26
Shore Fishing 42
Soft Weigh Sling 14
Spade End Hooks to Nylon 6
Spinners and Spoons 27
Split Shot, Non-toxic 7
Stillwater, Small 34
Swans 36
Sweetcorn 22
Swimfeeder 18
Swing Tip 17
Swivel 19
Tench 33
Trout Fishery, Small 37
Trout, Brown 40
Trout, Rainbow 41
Unhooking Mat 14
Waders 20
Weighing Scales 13
Weights, Carp 8
Weights, Non-toxic Ledger 7
Weights, Olivetti Pole 8
Weir Pool 35
Wire Trace 19
Worm, Lug 44
Worms 21
Wrasse 47

Answers
Ledger Rod: Quiver Tip.
Carp Rods: Split Cane.
Fixed Spool Reel: True.
Balsa and Avon Floats: True.
Swing Tip: False.
Swimfeeder: Yes.
Plugs: Yes.
Pike: True.
Common Carp: Redmire Pool.
Small Trout Fishery: True.
Trout Flies: True.
Mackerel: A Joey.

© I-Spy Limited 1997

ISBN 1 85671 180 3

Michelin Tyre Public Limited Company
Edward Hyde Building, 38 Clarendon Road, Watford,
Herts WD1 1SX

MICHELIN and the Michelin Man are Registered Trademarks of Michelin

All rights reserved. No part of this publication may be reproduced, stored in a retrieval system, or transmitted in any form or by any means, electronic, mechanical photocopying or otherwise without the prior written permission of I-Spy Limited.

A CIP record for this title is available from the British Library.

Edited and designed by Curtis Garratt Limited, The Old Vicarage, Horton cum Studley, Oxford OX9 1BT

The Publisher gratefully acknowledges the contribution of Laurence Bulaitis/Laurence Photography who provided all of the photographs in this I-Spy book. The Publisher also wishes to acknowledge Laurence and Tracy Bulaitis who wrote the text. The authors wish to thank Graham Gammage and Tony Emery for their assistance during the photography for this I-Spy book.

Colour reproduction by Norwich Litho Services Limited.

Printed in Spain.